Turning
Strips &
Squares Into
Table Sets™

Designs by Pearl Louise Krush

HOUSE of
WHITE
BIRCHES

PUBLISHERS
SINCE 1947

Introduction

By Pearl Louise Krush

In no time at all you can stir up some fun and functional projects to decorate your kitchen or dining room. These projects may be used throughout the year. Choose to make table runners, place mats, pot holders, tea cozies or even rugs.

This book is filled with many different styles and designs that are sure to please you. All of the designs are made by using either 5" charm squares, 10" squares, 2½"-wide strips, fat quarters and limited fabric yardage.

Whether you choose to use these sets for yourself or give them as gifts for friends and family, you are sure to find pleasure in the making.

Table of Contents

*Cottage Charm
Collection,*
page 5

Bull's-Eye Block Collection,
page 25

*Strip Happy
Kitchen Collection,*
page 31

Cottage Charm Collection

This sweet collection of quilted kitchen items is made by using a collection of 5" floral-print charm squares.

Project Note
Use a ¼" seam allowance for all stitching. Sew all seams with right sides together.

Project Specifications
Skill Level: Beginner
Table Runner Size: 39½" x 17½"
Bun Warmer Size: 13½" x 18" before ties;
    fits 8" x 11" dish
Tea Cozy Size: 11½" x 11½"
Pot Holder Size: 9" x 9"

Materials
- 37–5" x 5" assorted print A squares
- ½ yard white tonal
- 1 yard coordinating stripe
- 1⅝ yards floral
- Thin cotton batting: 45" x 23" (table runner)
- High-loft batting: 14" x 18½" (bun warmer) and two 12" x 12" squares (tea cozy)
- 9½" x 9½" square flame-retardant batting for pot holder
- Matching and contrasting all-purpose thread
- Quilting thread
- ½ yard ¼"-wide elastic
- ¼ yard fusible web
- 1 yard rayon cord
- 8" x 11" glass baking dish
- Basic sewing tools and supplies

Cutting Instructions for Set
1. Cut eight 1½" by fabric width strips white tonal; subcut strips into (14) 5" B strips, six 16" C strips, two 38" D strips and two 18" E strips.

2. Cut the following from the floral: three 2¼" by fabric width strips for runner binding; one 45" x 23" rectangle for runner backing; one 9½" x 9½" square for pot holder backing; two 12" x 12" I squares for tea cozy.

3. Cut the following from the coordinating stripe: one 14" x 18½" F rectangle for bun warmer lining; two 1½" by fabric width G/H strips for bun warmer

ties and pot-holder hanger; two 12" x 12" J squares for tea cozy lining; and four 1½" x 12" K strips for tea cozy casings.

4. Trace appliqué shapes given onto the paper side of the fusible web; cut out shapes, leaving a margin around each shape.

5. Fuse shapes to the wrong side of fabrics as directed on patterns for color; cut out shapes on traced lines. Remove paper backing.

Table Runner
Completing the Table Runner
1. Arrange 21 A squares in three rows of seven in each row, mixing up the prints, scale of prints and color of prints until the desired arrangement is achieved.

2. Keeping the squares as arranged, join three A squares with two B strips as shown in Figure 1; press seams toward A. Repeat with remaining A squares to complete seven A-B rows.

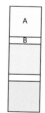

Figure 1

3. Join the A-B rows with C strips referring to the Placement Diagram for positioning to complete the pieced center; press seams toward C strips.

4. Sew D strips to opposite long sides and E strips to the short ends of the pieced center to complete the pieced top; press seams toward D and E strips.

Finishing the Table Runner
1. Sandwich batting between the completed top and prepared backing piece; pin or baste layers together to hold flat.

2. Quilt as desired by hand or machine; remove pins or basting. Trim batting and backing even with the top.

3. Join the binding strips with right sides together on short ends to make one long strip; press seams open.

4. Press the strip in half with wrong sides together along length.

5. Sew the binding to the right side of the runner edges, mitering corners and overlapping ends.

6. Fold binding to the back side and hand-stitch in place to finish.

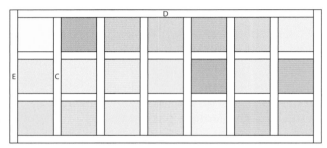

Cottage Charm Table Runner
Placement Diagram 39½" x 17½"

Bun Warmer

Completing the Bun Warmer

1. Arrange 12 A squares in three rows of four squares each, mixing up the prints, scale of prints and color of prints until the desired arrangement is achieved.

2. Join the four A squares as arranged to make a row; press seams in one direction. Repeat to make three rows, pressing seams in the center A row in the opposite direction from the other two rows.

3. Join the rows as arranged to complete the outside of the bun warmer (A unit).

4. Place the F rectangle right sides together with the A unit; place the layered unit with the A side on the 14" x 18½" rectangle high-loft batting; pin layers together at raw edges all around.

5. Sew all around outside edges, leaving a 4" opening on one side; clip corners. Trim batting close to seam.

6. Turn right side out through the opening; press.

7. Press opening edges to the inside ¼"; hand-stitch opening closed. Press again.

8. Machine-quilt in the ditch of seams.

9. Center the rectangular baking dish on the lining side of the stitched unit.

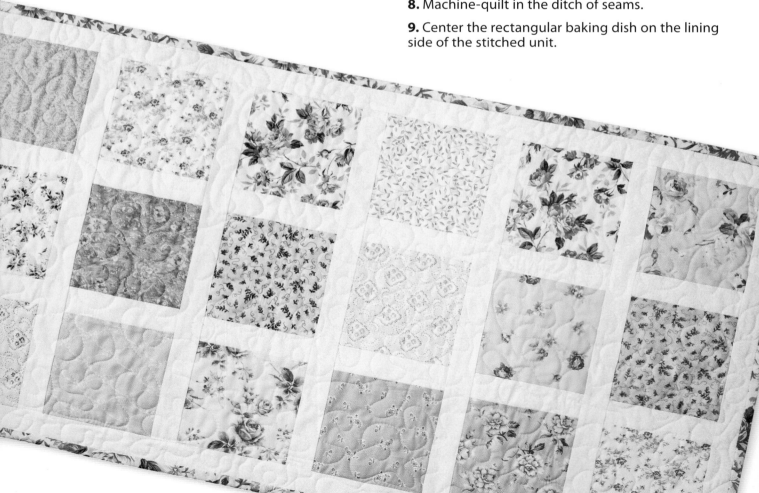

10. Pinch each corner of the stitched unit to fit the corners of the dish as shown in Figure 2; pin together and hand-stitch to secure corners together.

Figure 2

11. Referring to Figure 3, fold the long raw edges of the G/H strips to the center of the wrong side; press. Fold strips in half lengthwise and stitch along the double folded edge.

Figure 3

12. Cut the stitched strips into four equal 12" G/H strips and one 6½" H strip. Fold the raw ends in ¼" and stitch across ends to complete G ties. Set aside H strip for pot holder.

13. Tie a knot in the center of each G strip. Center the knot at each pinned corner of the stitched unit and hand-stitch in place to secure and to hold corners together.

14. Tie each G tie into a bow at each corner to complete the bun warmer.

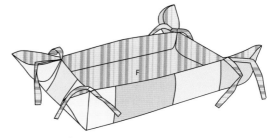

Cottage Charm Bun Warmer
Placement Diagram 13½" x 18", before ties

House of White Birches, Berne, Indiana 46711   DRGnetwork.com

Pot Holder

Complete the Pot Holder

1. Arrange four A squares in two rows of two squares each. Join the A squares to make two rows; press seams in opposite directions. Join the rows to complete the pot-holder background; press seam in one direction.

2. Center the teapot pieces diagonally on the pot-holder background, overlapping pieces as shown on pattern.

3. When satisfied with the arrangement, fuse shapes in place.

4. Using thread to match or contrast with pieces and a machine buttonhole stitch, sew around each shape.

5. Place the completed pot holder top right sides together with the 9½" x 9½" backing square and wrong side up on the 9½" x 9½" batting square; pin raw edges together.

6. Stitch all around, leaving a 4" opening on one side; clip corners. Trim batting close to seam.

7. Turn right side out through the opening; press.

8. Press opening edges to the inside ¼"; hand-stitch opening closed. Press again. Quilt as desired.

Figure 4

9. Fold the H strip to make a loop; hand-stitch loop ends to the back side of one corner of the stitched pot holder to complete as shown in Figure 4.

Cottage Charm Pot Holder
Placement Diagram 9" x 9"

Tea Cozy

Completing the Tea Cozy

1. Place an I square right sides together with a J square and place on one 12" x 12" square high-loft batting.

2. Stitch all around, leaving a 3" opening on one side; clip corners. Trim batting close to seam.

3. Turn right side out through the opening; press.

4. Press opening edges to the inside ¼"; hand-stitch opening closed. Press again.

5. Repeat steps 1–4 with remaining I and J pieces to make a second I-J unit.

6. Fold the long edges and ends of the K casing strips under ¼"; press.

7. Pin the pressed K strips on the J side of the stitched I-J units 1½" from two opposite edges as shown in Figure 5; stitch along the long edges of each strip, again referring to Figure 5.

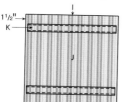

Figure 5

8. Place a safety pin in one end of the ¼"-wide elastic and thread through one casing of the I-J unit, out the other end and into the casing of the second I-J unit as shown in Figure 6; remove safety pin and stitch the ends of the elastic together to hold the I-J unit together at the bottom.

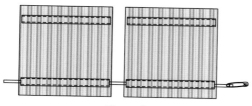

Figure 6

9. Trim the rayon cord to 30". Repeat step 8 with cord though the remaining casings; knot each end of the cord to finish.

10. Place cozy over teapot with elastic at bottom. Pull cord to tighten around teapot to use. ❖

Cottage Charm Tea Cozy
Placement Diagram 11½" x 11½"

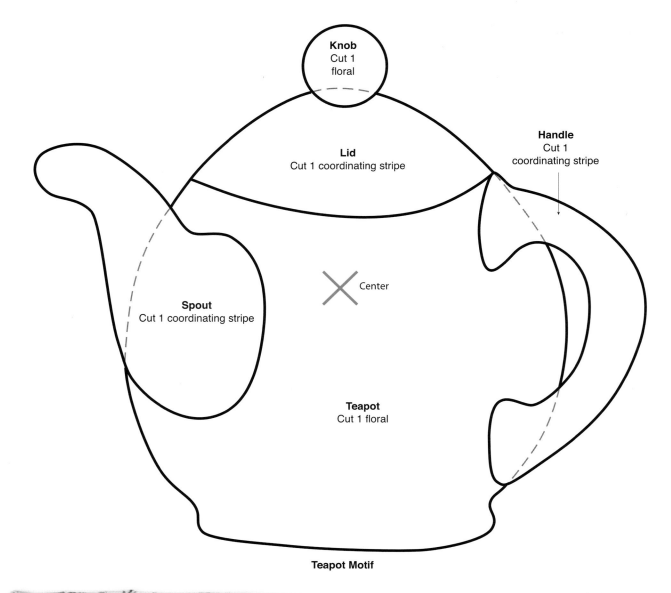

Knob
Cut 1
floral

Lid
Cut 1 coordinating stripe

Handle
Cut 1
coordinating stripe

Center

Spout
Cut 1 coordinating stripe

Teapot
Cut 1 floral

Teapot Motif

Summerset Fat Quarter Fancy Kitchen Collection

Sort your stash and find 15 coordinating fat quarters to create this colorful and easy-to-make set of place mats, coasters and napkins. Change the theme by changing the color palette for every season.

Project Note

Use a ¼" seam allowance for all stitching. Sew all seams with right sides together.

Project Specifications

Skill Level: Beginner
Place Mat Size: 18" x 12"
Napkin Size: 14" x 14"
Coaster Size: 4½" x 4½"

Materials

- 1 fat quarter each white and blue florals, yellow, blue, red and green tonals, and light blue print
- 4 coordinating fat quarters for backings
- 4 coordinating fat quarters for napkins
- 1⅝ yards coordinating plaid
- 1 yard thin cotton batting
- All-purpose thread to match coordinating plaid
- Basic sewing tools and supplies

Cutting Instructions for Set

1. From white floral, cut four 4½" x 4½" A squares for place mat centers and four 5" x 5" H squares for coasters.

2. Cut one 4½" x 21" strip yellow tonal; subcut strip into eight 2½" B strips.

3. Cut one 8½" x 21" strip light blue print; subcut strip into eight 2½" C strips.

4. Cut one 8½" x 21" strip red tonal; subcut strip into eight 2½" D strips.

5. Cut one 12½" x 21" strip blue tonal; subcut strip into eight 2½" E strips.

6. Cut one 12½" x 21" strip green tonal; subcut strip into eight 1½" F strips.

7. Cut one 12½" x 21" strip blue floral; subcut strip into eight 2½" G strips.

8. Cut four 21" x 15" place mat backings from assorted coordinating fat quarters.

9. Cut one 14½" x 14½" square each four coordinating fat quarters and four coordinating plaid for napkins.

10. Cut four 5" x 5" squares coordinating plaid for coaster backings.

11. Cut four 21" x 15" rectangles and four 5" x 5" squares batting.

12. Cut (10) 2¼" by fabric width strips coordinating plaid for binding for all projects.

Place Mats

Completing the Place Mats

1. Fold each 21" x 15" backing piece vertically and horizontally and crease to mark the centers.

2. Lay a 21" x 15" backing rectangle wrong side up on a flat surface; place a same-size batting piece on top.

3. Fold A and crease to mark the center; center A on the batting/backing layer, pinning through the center of A to the creased center of the backing; pin to hold in place.

4. Place a B strip right sides together on the top and bottom of A and stitch as shown in Figure 1; press B to the right side. ***Note:*** *Be careful when pressing; if batting is not heat-resistant, do not touch iron on batting.*

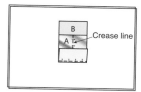

Figure 1

5. Repeat step 4 with C strips on opposite sides of A.

6. Repeat step 4 with D strips on the top and bottom.

7. Continue adding E, F and G strips to opposite sides to complete the pieced top.

8. Trim stitched top to 18½" x 12½".

9. Repeat steps 1–8 to complete four place mats.

10. Join binding strips on short ends with angled seams to make one long strip as shown in Figure 2; trim seam to ¼". Press seams open.

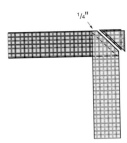

¼"

Figure 2

11. Fold strip with wrong sides together along length; press.

12. Pin binding to the right side of a place mat with raw edges even; stitch all around overlapping at the beginning and end; trim excess to set aside for binding other projects.

13. Turn binding to the back side; hand-stitch binding in place to finish.

14. Repeat binding steps to complete four place mats.

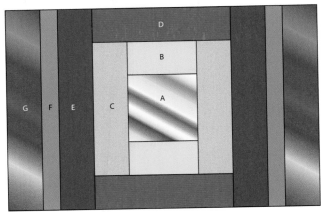

Summerset Fat Quarter Fancy Place Mat
Placement Diagram 18" x 12"

Napkins
Completing the Napkins

1. Lay a fat quarter napkin square right sides together with a coordinating plaid napkin square; stitch all around, leaving a 4" opening on one side.

2. Clip corners; turn right side out through opening.

3. Press opening edges ¼" to the inside; hand-stitch opening closed to complete one napkin.

4. Repeat steps 1–3 to complete four napkins.

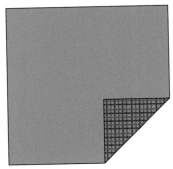

Summerset Fat Quarter Fancy Napkin
Placement Diagram 14" x 14"

Coasters
Completing the Coasters

1. Sandwich a 5" x 5" batting square between a same-size backing square and an H square; pin to hold layers together.

2. Bind edges as for place mats to complete.

3. Repeat steps 1 and 2 to complete four coasters. ❖

Summerset Fat Quarter Fancy Coaster
Placement Diagram 4½" x 4½"

Warm Winter Collection

Combine fat quarters with some yardage to create this fun and functional collection of kitchen accessories.

Project Note
Use a ¼" seam allowance for all stitching. Sew all seams with right sides together.

Project Specifications
Skill Level: Beginner
Table Runner Size: 43½" x 15¾"
Rug Size: 34" x 20½"
Pot Holder Size: 6" x 8¾"

Materials
- 1 fat quarter blue star print
- 1 fat quarter aqua star print
- ¼ yard cream tonal
- ⅜ yard brown print
- ½ yard burgundy tonal
- ⅞ yard coordinating plaid
- 2¼ yards brown tonal
- 2 yards thin cotton batting
- 12" x 14" piece flame-retardant batting
- Matching and contrasting all-purpose thread
- Quilting thread
- ½ yard fusible web
- 34" x 19" nonslip rug material
- Basic sewing tools and supplies

Cutting Instructions for Set
1. Cut two 10" x 10" A squares and two 7" x 8" N rectangles aqua star print.

2. Cut one 10" by fabric width strip brown print; subcut strip into two 10" x 10" B squares and two 8" x 10" M rectangles.

3. Cut three 1½" by fabric width strips cream tonal; subcut strips into two each 9¼" C, 11¼" E and 37" D.

4. Cut three 1" by fabric width strips burgundy tonal; subcut strips into two each 39" F and 12¼" G.

5. Cut one 5" by fabric width strip burgundy tonal; subcut strip into two 8" O rectangles and two 4" x 10" L rectangles.

6. Cut one 40" x 26" rug backing and one 49" x 22" runner backing from brown tonal.

7. Cut two 10" K squares brown tonal.

8. Cut three 2½" by fabric width strips coordinating plaid; subcut strips into two each 40" H strips and 16¼" I strips.

9. Cut seven 2¼" by fabric width strips coordinating plaid for runner, rug and pot holder binding, and pot holder hanging loop strips.

10. Cut two 9" x 10" J rectangles blue star print.

11. Trace small mitten and cuff, and large cuff appliqué pieces given onto the paper side of the fusible web; cut out shapes, leaving a margin around each shape.

12. Fuse shapes to the wrong side of fabrics as directed on patterns for color; cut out shapes on traced lines. Remove paper backing.

13. Prepare template for large mitten; cut as directed.

Table Runner
Completing the Pieced Center
1. Draw a diagonal line from corner to corner on the wrong side of each A square.

2. Layer an A square right sides together with a B square; stitch ¼" on each side of the marked line as shown in Figure 1. Cut apart on the marked line to make two A-B units, again referring to Figure 1; press seams toward B. Repeat with the remaining A and B squares.

Figure 1

3. Draw a diagonal line from corner to corner on the wrong side of two A-B units across the previously stitched seam as shown in Figure 2.

Figure 2

4. Layer one marked and one unmarked A-B unit, offsetting the placement of the pieces as shown in Figure 3.

Figure 3

5. Stitch ¼" on each side of the marked line as shown in Figure 4; cut apart on the marked lines to complete two B-A units, again referring to Figure 4. Press seams in one direction.

Figure 4

House of White Birches, Berne, Indiana 46711 DRGnetwork.com

Figure 6

9. Add an A-B-A unit to each end of the stitched unit to complete the pieced center as shown in Figure 7; press seams away from the A-B-A units. *Note: Some of the tip of the B piece will be caught in the seam; this will be covered with the cuff appliqué.*

Figure 7

Completing the Runner Top

1. Arrange and fuse one small mitten motif matching the marked X on pattern with the center seam of each of the two end B-A units as shown in Figure 8. Place a small cuff on each mitten as shown and fuse in place.

Figure 8

2. Using white thread and a machine buttonhole stitch, machine-stitch fused shapes in place.

3. Sew D strips to opposite long sides; press seams toward D. Sew E strips to the short ends of the pieced center; press seams toward E strips.

4. Sew F strips to opposite long sides and G strips to the short ends of the pieced center; press seams toward F and G strips.

5. Sew H strips to opposite long sides and I strips to the short ends of the pieced center to complete the pieced top; press seams toward H and I strips.

6. Repeat steps 4 and 5 to complete four B-A units.

7. Cut one B-A unit in half through the center to make two A-B-A units as shown in Figure 5.

A-B-A Units

Figure 5

8. Join three B-A units with two C strips as shown in Figure 6; press seams in one direction.

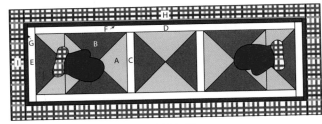

Warm Winter Table Runner
Placement Diagram 43½" x 15¾"

Finishing the Table Runner

1. Sandwich batting between the completed top and prepared backing piece; pin or baste layers together to hold flat.

2. Quilt as desired by hand or machine; remove pins or basting. Trim batting and backing even with the top.

3. Join the binding strips with right sides together on short ends to make one long strip; press seams open.

4. Press the strip in half with wrong sides together along length.

5. Sew the binding to the right side of the runner edges, mitering corners and overlapping ends. Trim excess and set aside for pot holders and rug.

6. Fold binding to the back side and hand-stitch in place to finish.

Pot Holders

Completing the Pot Holders

1. Fuse a large cuff piece to the top of one each blue and brown large mitten shape.

2. Using white thread and a machine buttonhole stitch, machine-stitch along seam between cuff and mitten.

3. Place a fused mitten shape and a same-color reversed mitten shape right sides together on top of one batting shape; stitch all around, leaving a 3½" opening on the cuff edge.

4. Clip curves every ¼" almost to the stitched seam as shown in Figure 9; trim batting layer close to seam.

5. Turn right side out through the opening; press edges flat. Hand-stitch opening closed.

6. Cut a 12" strip prepared binding. Pin the raw edge of the binding strip right sides together around the edge of the cuff. Trim binding ends ½" longer at bottom edge of cuffs and turn binding ends in. Machine-stitch the binding around the cuff. Turn binding to the wrong side and hand-stitch in place.

7. Cut one 5" length of prepared binding; unfold and press flat. Fold each short raw end ¼" to the wrong side and press.

8. Referring to Figure 10, fold the raw edges of the strip to the center of the wrong side; press. Fold strip in half and stitch along the double folded edge, and across the ends.

Figure 10

9. Fold the strip to make a loop; hand-stitch loop ends to the back side of one corner of the stitched pot holder to complete as shown in Figure 11. *Note: Loop may be stitched in with the binding if a cleaner look is desired.*

Figure 11

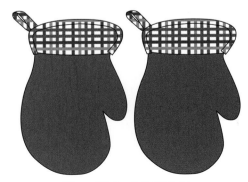

Warm Winter Pot Holders
Placement Diagram 6" x 8¾"

House of White Birches, Berne, Indiana 46711   DRGnetwork.com

10. Repeat steps 3–9 to complete a second pot holder.

11. Machine-quilt pot holders as desired to finish.

Rug

Completing the Rug

1. Sew J to K to L on the 10" sides; press seams toward J. Repeat to make two J-K-L units.

2. Sew M to N to O on the 8" sides; press seams toward M. Repeat to make two M-N-O units.

3. Join the pieced units to complete the pieced top referring to the Placement Diagram for positioning of units; press seams in one direction.

4. Arrange and fuse one small mitten and cuff on each N rectangle referring to the Placement Diagram for positioning.

5. Using white thread and a machine buttonhole stitch, machine-stitch fused shapes in place.

Finishing the Rug

1. Sandwich batting between the completed top and prepared backing piece; pin or baste layers together to hold flat.

2. Quilt as desired by hand or machine; remove pins or basting. Trim batting and backing even with the top.

3. Sew the binding left over from the runner to the right side of the rug edges, mitering corners and overlapping ends. Trim excess and set aside for pot holders.

4. Fold binding to the back side and hand-stitch in place to finish.

5. Place nonslip material under rug on floor to use. ❖

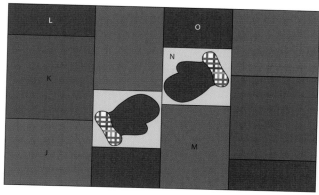

Warm Winter Rug
Placement Diagram 34" x 20½"

House of White Birches, Berne, Indiana 46711   DRGnetwork.com

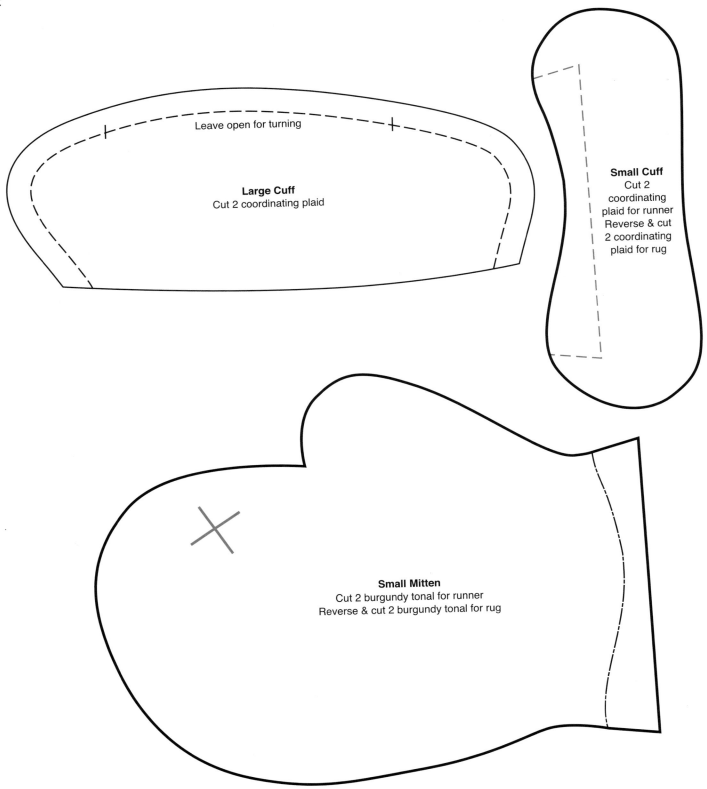

Leave open for turning

Large Cuff
Cut 2 coordinating plaid

Small Cuff
Cut 2
coordinating
plaid for runner
Reverse & cut
2 coordinating
plaid for rug

Small Mitten
Cut 2 burgundy tonal for runner
Reverse & cut 2 burgundy tonal for rug

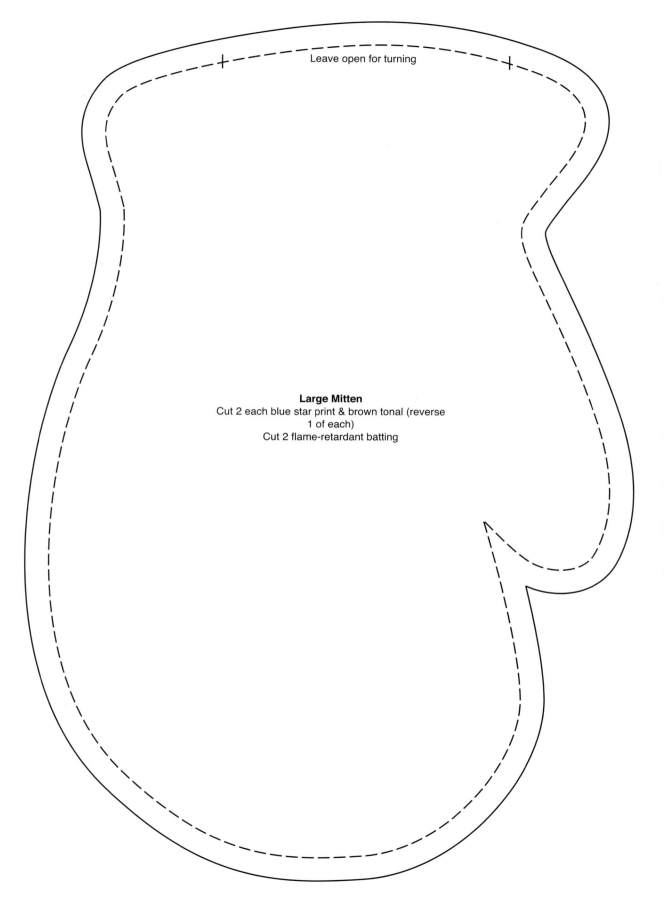

Leave open for turning

Large Mitten
Cut 2 each blue star print & brown tonal (reverse
1 of each)
Cut 2 flame-retardant batting

Bull's-Eye Block Collection

Simple circles of fabrics that fray easily make this collection deliciously different and easy to create. The rug, table runner and pot holders will look homespun happy in your home.

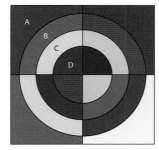

Bull's-Eye
8" x 8" Block
Make 11

Project Note

Use a ¼" seam allowance for all stitching. Sew all seams with right sides together.

Project Specifications

Skill Level: Beginner
Table Runner Size: 38¼" x 12¾"
Rug Size: 36" x 18"
Pot Holder Size: 8" diameter
Block Size: 8" x 8"
Number of Blocks: 11

Materials

- 11 fat quarters homespun plaids
- 1 fat quarter tan homespun
- 2⅜ yards tan homespun stripe
- 10" x 18" flame-retardant batting
- Batting 42" x 24" for rug and 44" x 19" for runner
- Matching or contrasting all-purpose thread
- Quilting thread
- Nonslip rug material
- Basic sewing tools and supplies

Cutting Instructions for Set

1. Cut one 10" x 10" A square from each of the 11 fat quarters.

2. Cut one 13" x 13" square tan homespun; cut the square on both diagonals to make four E triangles.

3. Prepare templates for B, C and D circle pieces using patterns given; cut as directed on each piece.

4. Cut six 2¼" by fabric width strips tan homespun stripe for rug and runner bindings.

5. Cut one backing piece each 42" x 24" for rug and 44" x 19" for runner from tan homespun stripe.

6. Cut and join 2¼" bias strips from tan homespun stripe to total 75" for pot holder binding as shown in Figure 1.

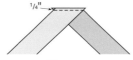

Figure 1

Completing the Blocks

1. Fold each A square and B, C and D circle and crease to mark the centers as shown in Figure 2.

Figure 2

2. Center a B circle on an A square, matching the creased lines as shown in Figure 3.

Figure 3

3. Sew ¼" inside the outer edge of B to sew B to A as shown in Figure 4.

Figure 4

4. Carefully pull the back layer of the A fabric away from B and trim out the center of the circle about ¼" from the stitching line to reduce bulk.

5. Repeat steps 2–4 with remaining A and B pieces, mixing fabrics to vary combinations.

6. Repeat steps 2–4 with C circles and then D circles to complete 11 circle units as shown in Figure 5.

Figure 5

7. Using the creased lines as guides, cut each circle unit into four equal A units as shown in Figure 6.

Figure 6

8. Shuffle the A units around; select four units. Join two units to make a row as shown in Figure 7; repeat to make two rows. Press seams in opposite directions.

Figure 7

9. Join the rows to complete one Bull's-Eye block referring to the block drawing; repeat to make 11 blocks. Press seams to one side.

Table Runner

Completing the Runner Top

1. Arrange and join three Bull's-Eye blocks with E in diagonal rows as shown in Figure 8; press seams toward E.

Figure 8

2. Join the diagonal rows to complete the pieced top; press seams in one direction.

Finishing the Runner

1. Sandwich batting between the completed top and prepared backing piece; pin or baste layers together to hold flat.

2. Quilt as desired by hand or machine; remove pins or basting. Trim batting and backing even with the top. *Note: The runner was machine-quilted in a 1" diagonal grid in the E triangles and in the ditch of unit-joining seams in the blocks.*

3. Join the binding strips with right sides together on short ends to make one long strip; press seams open.

4. Press the strip in half with wrong sides together along length.

5. Sew the binding to the runner edges, mitering corners and overlapping ends. Trim excess and set aside for rug binding.

6. Fold binding to the back side and stitch in place to finish.

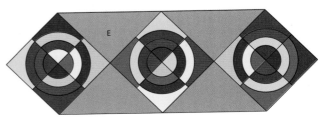

Bull's-Eye Block Runner
Placement Diagram 38¼" x 12¾"

Turning Strips & Squares Into Table Sets

Rug

Completing the Rug Top

1. Arrange eight blocks in two rows of four blocks each.

2. When satisfied with positioning, join the blocks in rows; press seams in opposite directions.

3. Join the rows to complete the pieced top; press seam in one direction.

Finishing the Rug

1. Sandwich batting between the completed top and prepared backing piece; pin or baste layers together to hold flat.

2. Quilt as desired by hand or machine; remove pins or basting. Trim batting and backing even with the top.

3. Sew the binding leftover from the runner to the rug edges, mitering corners and overlapping ends.

4. Fold binding to the back side and stitch in place to finish.

5. Place nonslip material under rug on floor to use.

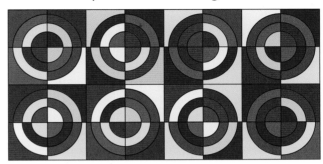

Bull's-Eye Block Rug
Placement Diagram 36" x 18"

Pot Holders

Completing the Pot Holder

1. Center one each C and D circles on B; pin to hold. Repeat to make a second layered unit.

2. Sandwich a batting circle between the two layered units; pin to hold.

3. Machine-stitch ¼" inside the edge of each C and D circle on one side of the layered unit to attach layers together.

4. Fold the 75" bias binding strip in half with wrong sides together along length; press.

5. Match raw edges of binding with raw edges of the stitched unit; sew all around, overlapping at the beginning and end to complete one pot holder.

6. Repeat steps 1–5 to complete a second pot holder. ❖

Bull's-Eye Pot Holder
Placement Diagram 8" diameter

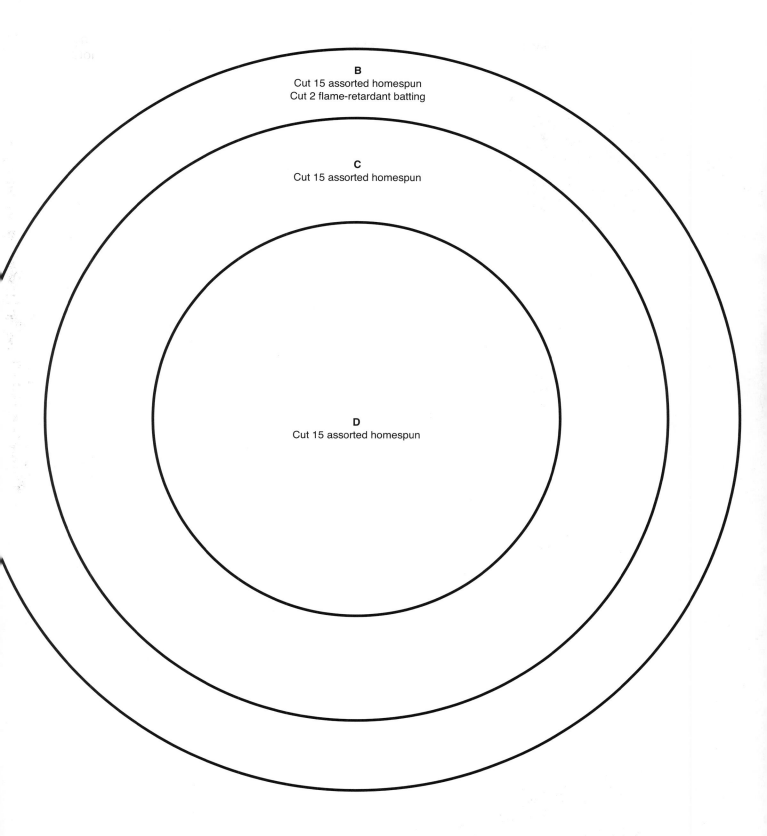

B
Cut 15 assorted homespun
Cut 2 flame-retardant batting

C
Cut 15 assorted homespun

D
Cut 15 assorted homespun

Strip Happy Kitchen Collection

Use up that stash by cutting 2½" strips. The coordinating fabric strips are sewn together in a "quilt-as-you-go" fashion. In no time at all you will have a collection of four place mats, two pot holders and a casserole cover.

Project Note
Use a ¼" seam allowance for all stitching. Sew all seams with right sides together.

Project Specifications
Skill Level: Beginner
Place Mat Size: 18½" x 12"
Casserole Cover: 28½" x 28½"
Pot Holder Size: 8½" x 6¼"

Materials
- 6 coordinating fat quarters
- 1½ yards coordinating binding fabric
- 2¼ yards backing fabric
- 2 yards batting
- 2 (8" x 10") rectangles flame-retardant batting
- Matching or contrasting all-purpose thread
- Quilting thread
- ⅓ yard heavyweight fusible interfacing or 9" x 9" square heavyweight cardboard
- 8½" x 9½" x 3" casserole dish
- 1 yard matching hook-and-loop tape
- Basic sewing tools and supplies

Cutting Instructions for Set
1. Cut the six fat quarters into 2½" x 18" C strips.

2. Cut four each 21" x 15" place-mat backing and batting rectangles.

3. Cut two each 14" x 32" casserole cover backing and batting rectangles.

4. Cut two 9" x 9" squares heavyweight fusible interfacing or one 9" x 9" square heavyweight cardboard for casserole cover.

5. Cut two 10" x 8" pot holder backing and backing rectangles.

6. Cut and join 2¼" bias strips to total 525" for binding for all projects.

Place Mats
Completing the Place Mats
1. Fold each batting rectangle in half to mark the centers as shown in Figure 1.

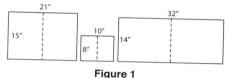
Figure 1

2. Prepare template for the angle pattern. Place the template on one 21" x 15" batting rectangle as shown in Figure 2; mark the angled edge on the batting, again referring to Figure 2.

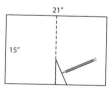
Figure 2

3. Place a long straightedge on the marked line to continue the line to the top edge of the batting rectangle as shown in Figure 3.

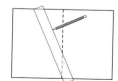
Figure 3

House of White Birches, Berne, Indiana 46711   DRGnetwork.com

4. Repeat steps 2 and 3 with all rectangles.

5. Lay a 21" x 15" batting rectangle on the wrong side of a same-size backing piece.

6. Place one C strip right side up on the center of the batting side of the layered rectangles with one edge aligned with the marked line as shown in Figure 4; place a second C strip right sides together with the first strip and stitch along one raw edge, again referring to Figure 4.

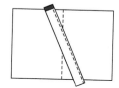

Figure 4

7. Press the top C strip to the right side as shown in Figure 5. *Note: Be very careful when pressing; if batting is not heat resistant, do not use an iron—finger-press instead.*

Figure 5

8. Continue adding C pieces to both sides of the first C piece until the entire surface is covered as shown in Figure 6; press after each addition.

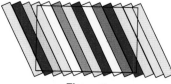

Figure 6

9. Prepare a template for the place mat oval using the pattern given. Center the template on the stitched unit and cut one oval-shaped place mat as shown in Figure 7.

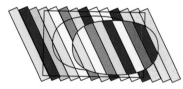

Figure 7

10. Repeat steps 5–9 to complete four place mats.

11. Join the binding strips with right sides together on short ends to make one long strip as shown in Figure 8; press seams open.

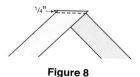

¼"

Figure 8

12. Press the strip in half with wrong sides together along length.

13. Place binding raw edges on the right side of a place mat; stitch all around overlapping at beginning and end, trimming excess to set aside for binding other projects.

14. Fold binding to the back side and hand-stitch in place to finish.

15. Repeat steps 13 and 14 to bind all place mats.

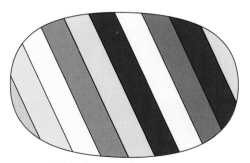

Strip Happy Kitchen Place Mat
Placement Diagram 18½" x 12"

Casserole Cover
Completing the Cover
1. Lay a 14" x 32" backing rectangle wrong side up on a flat surface; place a same-size batting rectangle on top.

2. Cover with C strips as in steps 6–8 for Completing the Place Mats.

3. Repeat steps 1 and 2 to complete two layered units.

4. Trim each layered unit to 10" x 28".

5. Bind edges of each layered unit with leftover bias binding referring to steps 13 and 14 for Completing the Place Mats.

6. Fold each bound rectangle in half to find the center as shown in Figure 9; crease.

Figure 9

7. Center one bound rectangle on top of the other as shown in Figure 10; pin along three side edges to secure.

Figure 10

8. Double-stitch around the three sides as shown in Figure 11.

Figure 11

9. Insert the 9" x 9" squares heavyweight interfacing or the cardboard square into the pocket through the open side.

10. Cut the hook-and-loop tape into four 9" strips.

11. Pin a hook strip close to the bound edge on the wrong side of one rectangle and the loop strip 3" from the bound edge on the right side of the opposite end of the same rectangle as shown in Figure 12; hand- or machine-stitch in place. *Note: Before stitching in place, place casserole dish in the center and bring ends over to be sure the loop strip is positioned correctly for your dish.*

3"

Figure 12

12. Repeat step 11 on the remaining rectangle.

13. Place a casserole dish in the center and fold ends of rectangles over the dish and secure with hook-and-loop tape to use.

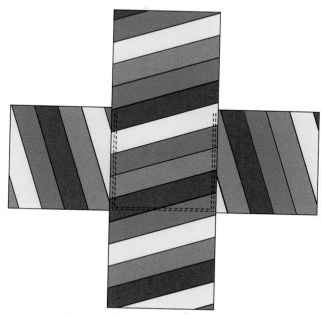

Strip Happy Kitchen Casserole Cover
Placement Diagram 28½" x 28½"

Pot Holders

Completing the Pot Holders

1. Repeat steps 6–9 and steps 13 and 14 for place mats using the 8" x 10" backing and flame-retardant batting pieces and the pot holder oval pattern to complete two pot holders. ❖

Strip Happy Kitchen Pot Holder
Placement Diagram 8½" x 6¼"

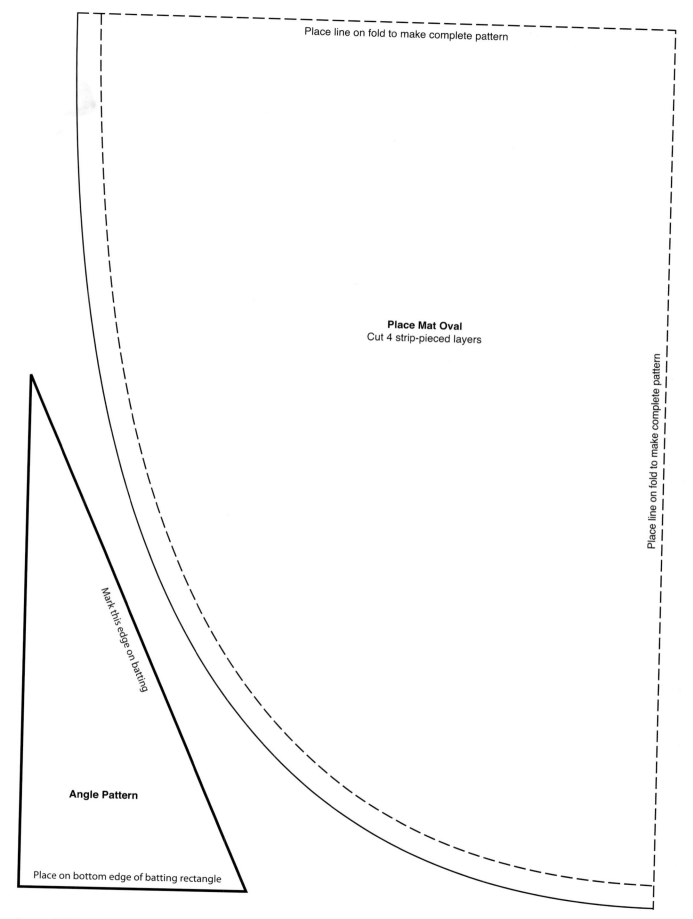

37

Place line on fold to make complete pattern

Place Mat Oval
Cut 4 strip-pieced layers

Place line on fold to make complete pattern

Mark this edge on batting

Angle Pattern

Place on bottom edge of batting rectangle

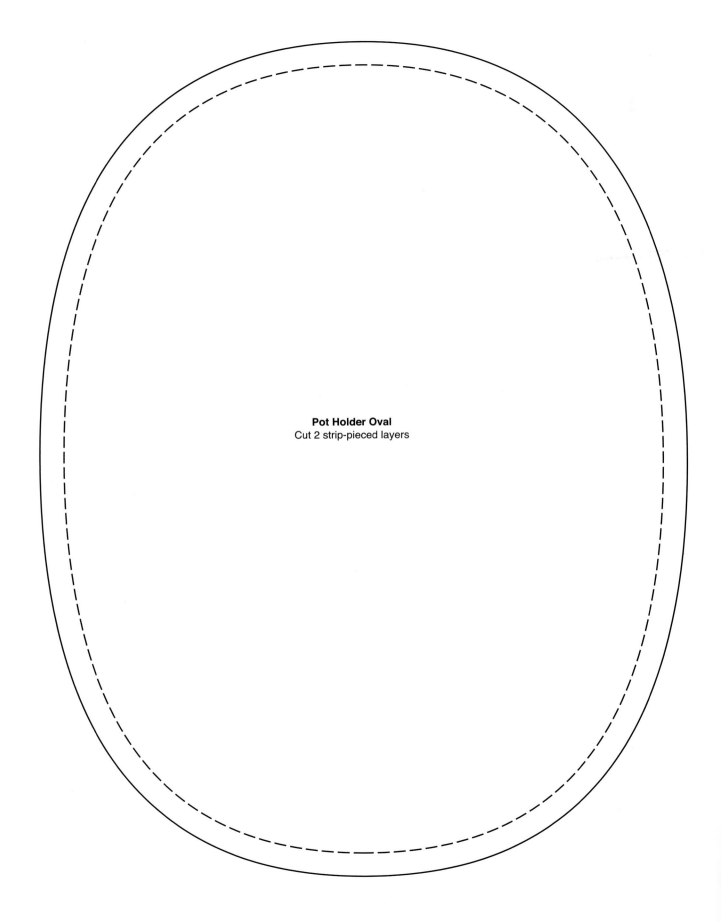

Pot Holder Oval
Cut 2 strip-pieced layers

Quiltmaking Basics

Materials & Supplies

Fabrics
Use 100 percent cotton fabrics.

Thread
Use good-quality cotton or cotton-covered polyester thread.

Batting
Batting gives a quilt loft or thickness. It also adds warmth. Purchase a size large enough to cut the size you need for your quilt.

Tools & Equipment
There are few truly essential tools and little equipment required for quiltmaking. Basics include needles (start with size 9 and adjust as you become more experienced), pins (long, thin, sharp pins are best), scissors, a thimble, template materials (plastic or cardboard), marking tools (chalk marker, water-erasable pen or a No. 2 pencil), a rotary cutter, cutting mat and ruler, and a quilting frame or hoop.

Construction Methods

Cutting
Quick Cutting. Many pieces for quilts can be cut using a rotary cutter with a plastic ruler and mat. To prepare fabric for quick cutting, follow the steps below.

1. Straighten raw edges of fabric by folding fabric in fourths across the width as shown in Figure 1.

2. Press down flat; place ruler on fabric square with edge of fabric and make one cut from the folded edge to the outside edge. If strips are not straightened,

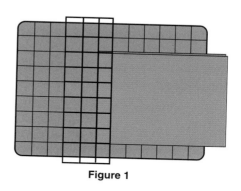

Figure 1

Figure 2

a wavy strip will result as shown in Figure 2. Always cut away from your body, holding the ruler firmly with the noncutting hand.

3. Follow the instructions given with each pattern for the size and number of cuts to make.

Traditional Templates. There are two types of templates: those that include a ¼" seam allowance (see Machine Piecing on page 40) and those that don't. For hand piecing and appliqué, use instructions below to cut out templates without seam allowances.

1. Place the template on the wrong side of the fabric.

2. Trace around shape.

3. Move template, leaving ½" between the shapes and mark again.

4. Cut out pieces, leaving ¼" beyond marked line all around each piece.

Piecing Basics

Hand Piecing

When joining two pieces by hand, it is easier to begin with templates that do not include the ¼" seam allowance. For accurate piecing, follow the instructions below.

1. To join two units, place the patches with right sides together.

2. Stick a pin in at the beginning of the seam through both fabric patches, matching the beginning points (Figure 3); the seam begins on the traced line, not at the edge of the fabric (Figure 4).

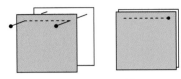

Figure 3   **Figure 4**

3. Thread a sharp needle; knot one strand of the thread at the end. Remove the pin and insert the needle in the hole; make a short stitch and then a backstitch right over the first stitch.

4. Continue making short stitches with several stitches on the needle at one time. As you stitch, check the back piece often.

5. Take a stitch at the end of the seam; backstitch and knot at the same time as shown in Figure 5.

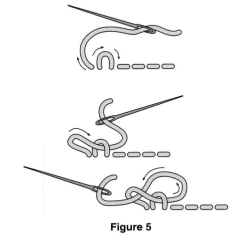

Figure 5

Machine Piecing

Include the ¼" seam allowance on the template for machine piecing.

1. Place template on the wrong side of the fabric

2. Trace around shape.

3. Move template, butting pieces against one another.

4. Cut out pieces.

5. Set machine on 2.5 or 12–15 stitches per inch. Join pieces as for hand piecing, beginning and ending sewing at the end of the fabric patch. No back-stitching is necessary when machine-stitching.

Appliqué Basics

Making Templates

Using a light box, transfer design to fabric background.

If you don't have a light box, tape the pattern on a window; center the background block on top and tape in place. Trace the design onto the background block with a No. 2 pencil. This drawing marks where the fabric pieces should be placed.

Hand Appliqué

Traditional hand appliqué uses a template made from the desired finished shape without the seam allowance added.

1. Trace the desired shape onto the right side of the fabric with marking tool. Leave at least ½" between design motifs when tracing to allow for the seam allowance when cutting out the shapes.

2. When the desired number of shapes needed has been drawn on the fabric pieces, cut out shapes leaving ⅛"–¼" all around drawn line for turning under.

3. Finger-press the shape's edges over on the drawn line. When turning in concave curves, clip to seams and baste the seam allowance over as shown in Figure 6.

Figure 6

4. Position the fabric shapes on the background block and pin them in place.

5. Using a blind stitch, sew pieces in place with matching thread and small stitches. Start with background pieces first and work up to foreground pieces.

Machine Appliqué

Fusible transfer web makes the machine-appliqué process easier. It is similar to iron-on interfacing, except it has two sticky sides. Using an iron, follow the instructions below to adhere the appliqué shapes to the background block.

1. Reverse pattern and draw shapes onto the paper side of the fusible web.

2. Cut, leaving a margin around each shape.

3. Place on the wrong side of the chosen fabric; fuse in place, referring to the manufacturer's instructions.

4. Cut out shapes on the drawn line.

5. Peel off the paper and fuse in place on the background fabric. Transfer any detail lines to the fabric shapes.

Finishing Basics

Choose a Quilting Design

If you choose to hand- or machine-quilt your finished top, you will need to choose a design for quilting.

There are several types of quilting designs, some of which may not have to be marked. The easiest of the unmarked designs is in-the-ditch quilting. Here the quilting stitches are placed in the valley created by the seams joining two pieces together or next to the edge of an appliqué design. There is no need to mark a top for in-the-ditch quilting. Machine quilters choose this option because the stitches are not as obvious on the finished quilt (Figure 1).

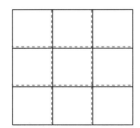

Figure 1
In-the-ditch quilting is done in
the seam that joins 2 pieces.

Outline-quilting ¼" or more away from seams or appliqué shapes is another no-mark alternative (Figure 2) which prevents having to sew through the layers made by seams, thus making stitching easier.

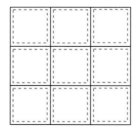

Figure 2
Outline-quilting ¼" away
from seam is a popular
choice for quilting.

If you are not comfortable eyeballing the ¼" (or other distance), masking tape is available in different widths and is helpful to place on straightedge designs to mark the quilting line. If using masking tape, place the tape right up against the seam and quilt close to the other edge.

Meander or free-motion quilting by machine fills in open spaces and doesn't require marking. It is fun and easy to stitch as shown in Figure 3.

Figure 3
Machine meander-quilting
fills in spaces.

Mark the Top for Quilting

If you choose a fancy or allover design for quilting, you will need to transfer the design to your quilt top before layering with the backing and batting. You may use a sharp medium-lead or silver pencil on light background fabrics. Test the pencil marks to guarantee that they will wash out of your quilt top when quilting is complete, or be sure your quilting stitches cover the pencil marks. Mechanical pencils with very fine points may be used successfully to mark quilts.

Manufactured quilt-design templates are available in many designs and sizes, and are cut out of a durable plastic template material that is easy to use.

To make a permanent quilt-design template, choose a template material on which to transfer the design. See-through plastic is the best choice as it will let you place the template while allowing you to see where it is in relation to your quilt design without moving it. Place the template on the quilt top where you want it and trace around it with your marking tool. Pick up the quilting template and place again; repeat marking.

No matter what marking method you use, remember, the marked lines should *never show* on the finished quilt. When the top is marked, it is ready for layering.

Prepare the Quilt Backing

The quilt backing is a very important feature of your quilt. In most cases, the materials list gives the size requirements for the backing, not the yardage needed.

A backing is generally cut at least 6" larger than the quilt top or 2" larger on all sides. For a 64" x 78" finished quilt, the backing would need to be at least 70" x 84".

Layer the Quilt Sandwich

Place the batting on top of the backing; flatten out any wrinkles. Trim the batting to the same size as the backing.

To hold the quilt layers together for quilting, baste by hand or use safety pins. If basting by hand, thread a long thin needle with a long piece of unknotted white or off-white thread. Starting in the center and leaving a long tail, make 4"–6" stitches toward the outside edge of the quilt top, smoothing as you baste. Start at the center again and work toward the outside as shown in Figure 4.

Figure 4
Baste from the center
to the outside edges.

If quilting by machine, you may prefer to use safety pins for holding your quilt sandwich together. Start in the center of the quilt and pin to the outside, leaving pins open until all are placed. When you are satisfied that all layers are smooth, close the pins.

Hand Quilting

Hand quilting is the process of placing stitches through the quilt top, batting and backing to hold them together. While it is a functional process, it also adds beauty and loft to the finished quilt.

To begin, thread a sharp between needle with an 18" piece of quilting thread. Tie a small knot in the end of the thread. Position the needle about ½" to 1" away from the starting point on quilt top. Sink the needle through the top into the batting layer but not through the backing. Pull the needle up at the starting point of the quilting design. Pull the needle and thread until the knot sinks through the top into the batting (Figure 5).

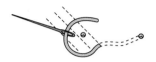

Figure 5
Start the needle through the top layer
of fabric ½"–1" away from quilting line
with knot on top of fabric.

Some stitchers like to take a backstitch at the beginning while others prefer to begin the first stitch here. Take small, even running stitches along the marked quilting line (Figure 6). Keep one hand positioned underneath to feel the needle go all the way through to the backing.

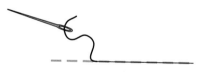

Figure 6
Make small, even running stitches
on marked quilting line.

Machine Quilting

Successful machine quilting requires practice and a good relationship with your sewing machine.

Prepare the quilt for machine quilting in the same way as for hand quilting. Use safety pins to hold the layers together instead of basting with thread.

Presser-foot quilting is best used for straight-line quilting because the presser bar lever does not need to be continually lifted.

Set the machine on a longer stitch length. Too tight a stitch causes puckering and fabric tucks, either on the quilt top or backing. An even-feed or walking foot helps to eliminate the tucks and puckering by feeding the upper and lower layers through the machine evenly. Before you begin, loosen the amount of pressure on the presser foot.

Special machine-quilting needles work best to penetrate the three layers in your quilt.

Decide on a design. Quilting in the ditch is not quite as visible, but if you quilt with the feed dogs engaged, it means turning the quilt frequently. It is not easy to fit a rolled-up quilt through the small opening on the sewing machine head.

Meander quilting is the easiest way to machine-quilt—and it is fun. Meander quilting is done using an appliqué or darning foot with the feed dogs dropped. It is sort of like scribbling. Simply move the quilt top around under the foot and make stitches in a random pattern to fill the space. The same method may be used to outline a quilt design. The trick is the same as in hand quilting; you are striving for stitches of uniform size. Your hands are in complete control of the design.

Quilting Tips

Use a thimble to prevent sore fingers when hand quilting. The finger that is under the quilt to feel the needle as it passes through the backing is the one that is most apt to get sore from the pin pricks. Some quilters purchase leather thimbles for this finger while others try home remedies. One simple aid is masking tape wrapped around the finger. With the tape you will still be able to feel the needle, but it will not prick your skin. Over time, calluses build up and these fingers get toughened up, but with every vacation from quilting, they will become soft, and the process begins again.

Knots should not show on the quilt top or back. Learn to sink the knot into the batting at the beginning and ending of the quilting thread for successful stitches.

When you have nearly run out of thread, wind the thread around the needle several times to make a small knot and pull it close to the fabric. Insert the needle into the fabric on the quilting line and come out with the needle ½" to 1" away, pulling the knot into the fabric layers the same as when you started. Pull and cut thread close to fabric. The end should disappear inside after cutting. Some quilters prefer to take a backstitch with a loop through it for a knot to end.

Making 12–18 stitches per inch is a nice goal, but a more realistic goal is seven to nine stitches per inch. If you cannot accomplish this right away, strive for even stitches—all the same size—that look as good on the back as on the front.

Meet the Designer

I simply love to design projects that make people smile. Even as a small child I enjoyed making things out of paper, clay and fabric.

As a young mother of three sons and the wife of a very busy husband I wanted to make a little extra money for all of the extras every family needs. One of the earliest businesses I created was a "Barbie Party." I would have my friends and other moms have a Barbie Party, and I would show a collection of doll clothes that I had designed. They would order what they wanted, and I would then deliver and charge for the wardrobes that had been ordered. It was a great learning experience.

In 1989, I started the Pearl Louise Designs pattern company and started showing my designs at the International Quilt Market. When my local quilt shop closed, I decided to open The Thimble Cottage Quilt Shop as I needed quilt-shop fabrics to make my designs. The quilt shop and my home are in Rapid City, S.D., just a few miles from Mount Rushmore. During the summer months, we are very busy with visitors from around the world, and I truly enjoy visiting with all of them. Over the years the shop has evolved into a place where customers can come and enjoy our collection of fabrics, classes and clubs that we offer as well as our Web store, www.thimblecottage. com. I began designing fabric for the Troy Corp. several years ago and have found it very interesting and challenging. Most of my designs are whimsical winter and baby designs, but now I'm venturing into designing a home decor collection, which should be tons of fun.

My husband, Fred, and I enjoy fishing in the summer months. We have two dogs—Bella and Kate, and Telly the bird. (Bella goes to the shop every day.) My sons are grown, and we now have two wonderful daughters-in-law and three charming grandchildren.

One of my very favorite sayings has always been "Happiness Is Homemade."

Enjoy!!

Pearl Louise Krush

Metric Conversion Charts

Metric Conversions

Canada/U.S. Measurement		Multiplied by		Metric Measurement
yards	x	.9144	=	metres (m)
yards	x	91.44	=	centimetres (cm)
inches	x	2.54	=	centimetres (cm)
inches	x	25.40	=	millimetres (mm)
inches	x	.0254	=	metres (m)

Canada/U.S. Measurement		Multiplied by		Metric Measurement
centimetres	x	.3937	=	inches
metres	x	1.0936	=	yards

Standard Equivalents

Canada/U.S. Measurement				Metric Measurement
⅛ inch	=	3.20 mm	=	0.32 cm
¼ inch	=	6.35 mm	=	0.635 cm
⅜ inch	=	9.50 mm	=	0.95 cm
½ inch	=	12.70 mm	=	1.27 cm
⅝ inch	=	15.90 mm	=	1.59 cm
¾ inch	=	19.10 mm	=	1.91 cm
⅞ inch	=	22.20 mm	=	2.22 cm
1 inches	=	25.40 mm	=	2.54 cm
⅛ yard	=	11.43 cm	=	0.11 m
¼ yard	=	22.86 cm	=	0.23 m
⅜ yard	=	34.29 cm	=	0.34 m
½ yard	=	45.72 cm	=	0.46 m
⅝ yard	=	57.15 cm	=	0.57 m
¾ yard	=	68.58 cm	=	0.69 m
⅞ yard	=	80.00 cm	=	0.80 m
1 yard	=	91.44 cm	=	0.91 m
1⅛ yard	=	102.87 cm	=	1.03 m
1¼ yard	=	114.30 cm	=	1.14 m

Canada/U.S. Measurement				Metric Measurement
1⅜ yard	=	125.73 cm	=	1.26 m
1½ yard	=	137.16 cm	=	1.37 m
1⅝ yard	=	148.59 cm	=	1.49 m
1¾ yard	=	160.02 cm	=	1.60 m
1⅞ yard	=	171.44 cm	=	1.71 m
2 yards	=	182.88 cm	=	1.83 m
2⅛ yards	=	194.31 cm	=	1.94 m
2¼ yards	=	205.74 cm	=	2.06 m
2⅜ yards	=	217.17 cm	=	2.17 m
2½ yards	=	228.60 cm	=	2.29 m
2⅝ yards	=	240.03 cm	=	2.40 m
2¾ yards	=	251.46 cm	=	2.51 m
2⅞ yards	=	262.88 cm	=	2.63 m
3 yards	=	274.32 cm	=	2.74 m
3⅛ yards	=	285.75 cm	=	2.86 m
3¼ yards	=	297.18 cm	=	2.97 m
3⅜ yards	=	308.61 cm	=	3.09 m
3½ yards	=	320.04 cm	=	3.20 m
3⅝ yards	=	331.47 cm	=	3.31 m
3¾ yards	=	342.90 cm	=	3.43 m
3⅞ yards	=	354.32 cm	=	3.54 m
4 yards	=	365.76 cm	=	3.66 m
4⅛ yards	=	377.19 cm	=	3.77 m
4¼ yards	=	388.62 cm	=	3.89 m
4⅜ yards	=	400.05 cm	=	4.00 m
4½ yards	=	411.48 cm	=	4.11 m
4⅝ yards	=	422.91 cm	=	4.23 m
4¾ yards	=	434.34 cm	=	4.34 m
4⅞ yards	=	445.76 cm	=	4.46 m
5 yards	=	457.20 cm	=	4.57 m

Fabric & Supplies

Page 16, Warm Winter Collection—
Dancing Under the Stars fabric collection by Pearl Louise Krush for Troy Riverwoods fabrics.

Page 31, Strip Happy Kitchen Collection—
Timtex interfacing

E-mail: Customer_Service@whitebirches.com

HOUSE of
WHITE
BIRCHES
PUBLISHERS
SINCE 1947

Turning Strips & Squares Into Table Sets is published by DRG, 306 East Parr Road, Berne, IN 46711, telephone (260) 589-4000. Printed in USA. Copyright © 2009 DRG. All rights reserved. This publication may not be reproduced in part or in whole without written permission from the publisher.

RETAIL STORES: If you would like to carry this pattern book or any other DRG publications, call the Wholesale Department at Annie's Attic to set up a direct account: (903) 636-4303. Also, request a complete listing of publications available from DRG.

Every effort has been made to ensure that the instructions in this pattern book are complete and accurate. We cannot, however, take responsibility for human error, typographical mistakes or variations in individual work.

STAFF

Editors: Jeanne Stauffer, Sandra L. Hatch
Managing Editor: Dianne Schmidt
Technical Artist: Connie Rand
Copy Supervisor: Michelle Beck
Copy Editors: Mary O'Donnell, Susanna Tobias
Graphic Arts Supervisor: Ronda Bechinski

Graphic Artists: Pam Gregory, Erin Augsburger
Art Director: Brad Snow
Assistant Art Director: Nick Pierce
Photography Supervisor: Tammy Christian
Photography: Matthew Owen
Photo Stylist: Tammy Steiner

ISBN: 978-1-59217-261-0
1 2 3 4 5 6 7 8 9

House of White Birches, Berne, Indiana 46711   DRGnetwork.com

Photo Index

16

5

25

11

31

21

27